All royalties from this book will be donated to

THE ERIC CARLE MUSEUM OF PICTURE BOOK ART,

which was founded by Eric and Barbara Carle to inspire a
love of art and reading through picture books.

Visit the Eric Carle Museum of Picture Book Art
in Amherst, Massachusetts, or at carlemuseum.org.

Permission to reproduce the following is gratefully acknowledged:
"Yellow" © 2017 by Eric Carle; "Blue" © 2017 by Bryan Collier; "Mint" © 2017 by Mike Curato; "Brown" © 2017 by William Low;
"Indigo" © 2017 by Etienne Delessert; "Purple" © 2017 by Anna Dewdney; "Gray" © 2017 by Rafael López;
"White" © 2017 by Lauren Castillo; "Green" © 2017 by Philip C. Stead; "Mexican Pink" © 2017 by Yuyi Morales;
"Maine Morning Gray" © 2017 by Melissa Sweet; "Orange" © 2017 by Frann Preston-Gannon;
"Black" © 2017 by Jill McElmurry; "Crimson Red" © 2017 by Marc Martin; "All Colors" © 2017 by Uri Shulevitz.

Henry Holt and Company, *Publishers since 1866*
175 Fifth Avenue, New York, New York 10010 • mackids.com

Henry Holt® is a registered trademark of Macmillan Publishing Group, LLC.
Compilation copyright © 2017 by Eric Carle
All rights reserved.

Library of Congress Control Number 2016953950
ISBN 978-0-8050-9614-9

Our books may be purchased in bulk for promotional, educational, or business use. Please contact your local bookseller or the
Macmillan Corporate and Premium Sales Department at (800) 221-7945 ext. 5442
or by e-mail at MacmillanSpecialMarkets@macmillan.com.

First edition—2017
Printed in China by RR Donnelley Asia Printing Solutions Ltd., Dongguan City, Guangdong Province

1 3 5 7 9 10 8 6 4 2

Eric Carle and Friends

What's Your Favorite Color?

Lauren Castillo • Bryan Collier • Mike Curato

Etienne Delessert • Anna Dewdney • Rafael López

William Low • Marc Martin • Jill McElmurry

Yuyi Morales • Frann Preston-Gannon

Uri Shulevitz • Philip C. Stead • Melissa Sweet

GODWIN BOOKS

Henry Holt and Company

NEW YORK

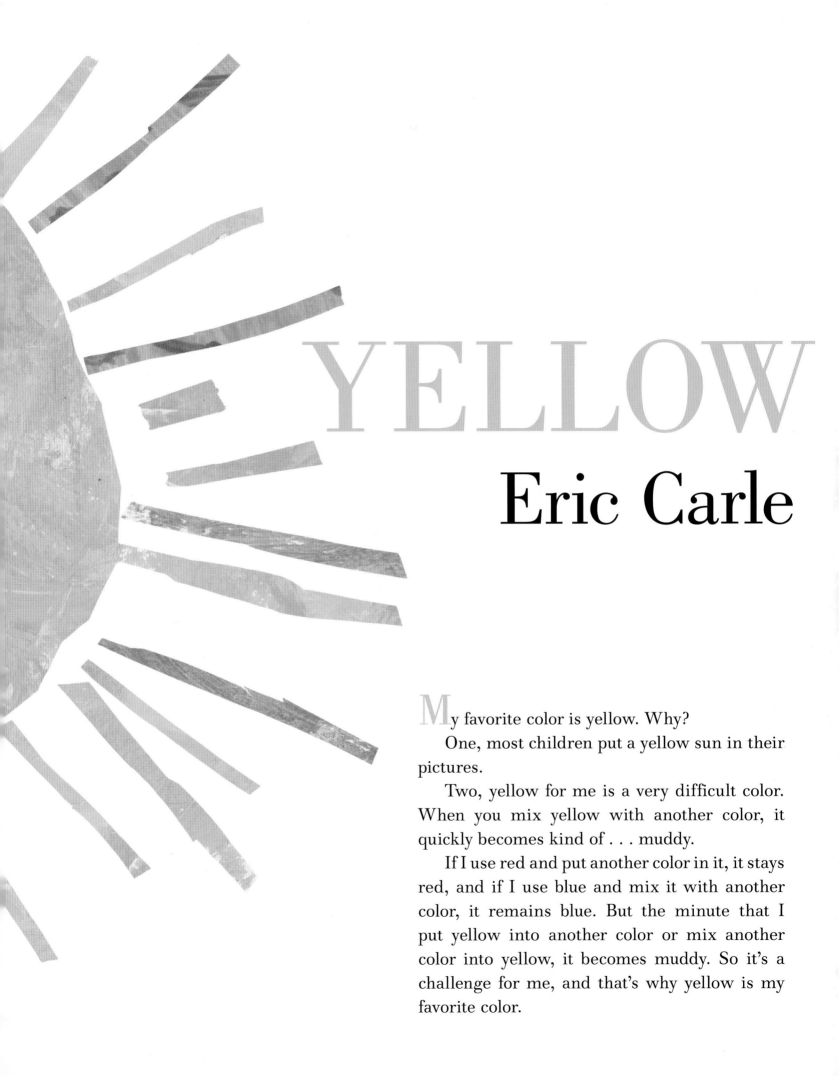

YELLOW
Eric Carle

My favorite color is yellow. Why?

One, most children put a yellow sun in their pictures.

Two, yellow for me is a very difficult color. When you mix yellow with another color, it quickly becomes kind of . . . muddy.

If I use red and put another color in it, it stays red, and if I use blue and mix it with another color, it remains blue. But the minute that I put yellow into another color or mix another color into yellow, it becomes muddy. So it's a challenge for me, and that's why yellow is my favorite color.

BLUE

Bryan Collier

Blue is my favorite color.

On rainy days—I call them blue days—I would buy a bunch of blue balloons for my daughter just to make her smile and brighten up the day.

I know there will always be rainy days. And my daughter still has the power to light up my world. But I still go out and buy balloons in bunches of blue.

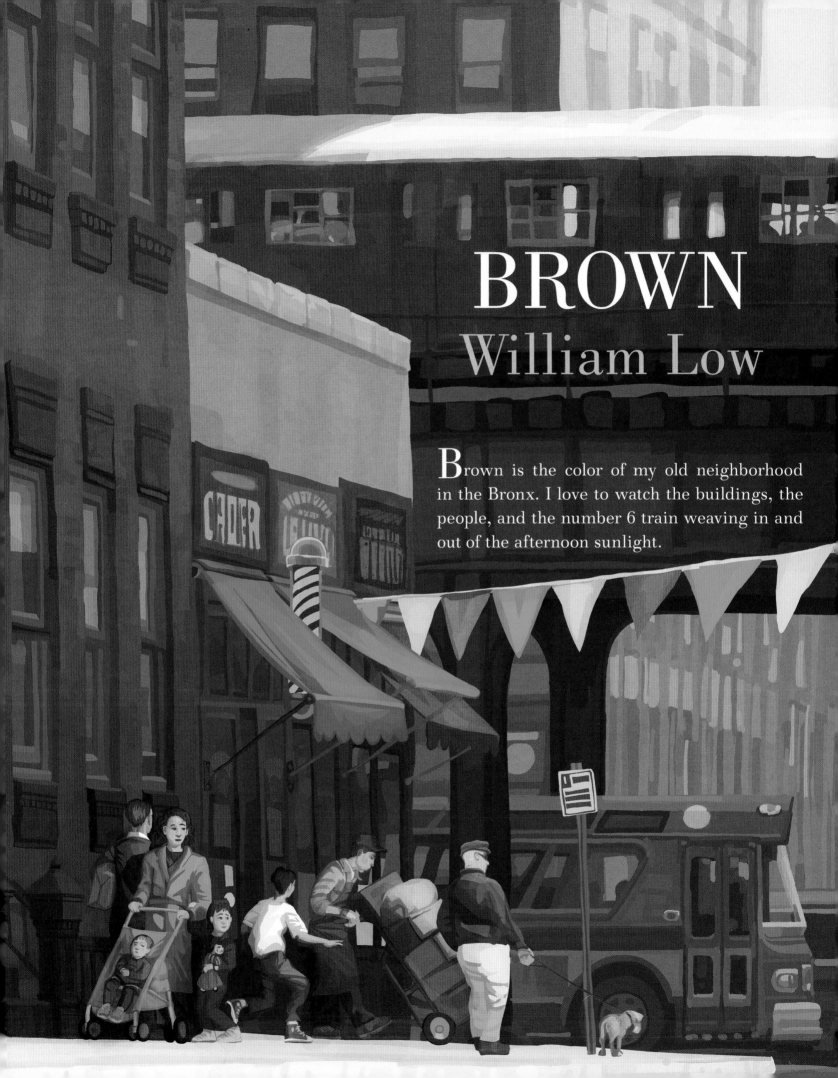

BROWN
William Low

Brown is the color of my old neighborhood in the Bronx. I love to watch the buildings, the people, and the number 6 train weaving in and out of the afternoon sunlight.

INDIGO

ETIENNE DELESSERT

The Tuareg nomads wear long cotton **INDIGO** veils.

They herd camels and goats
and talk to the spirits of the Sahara Desert.

PURPLE
Anna Dewdney

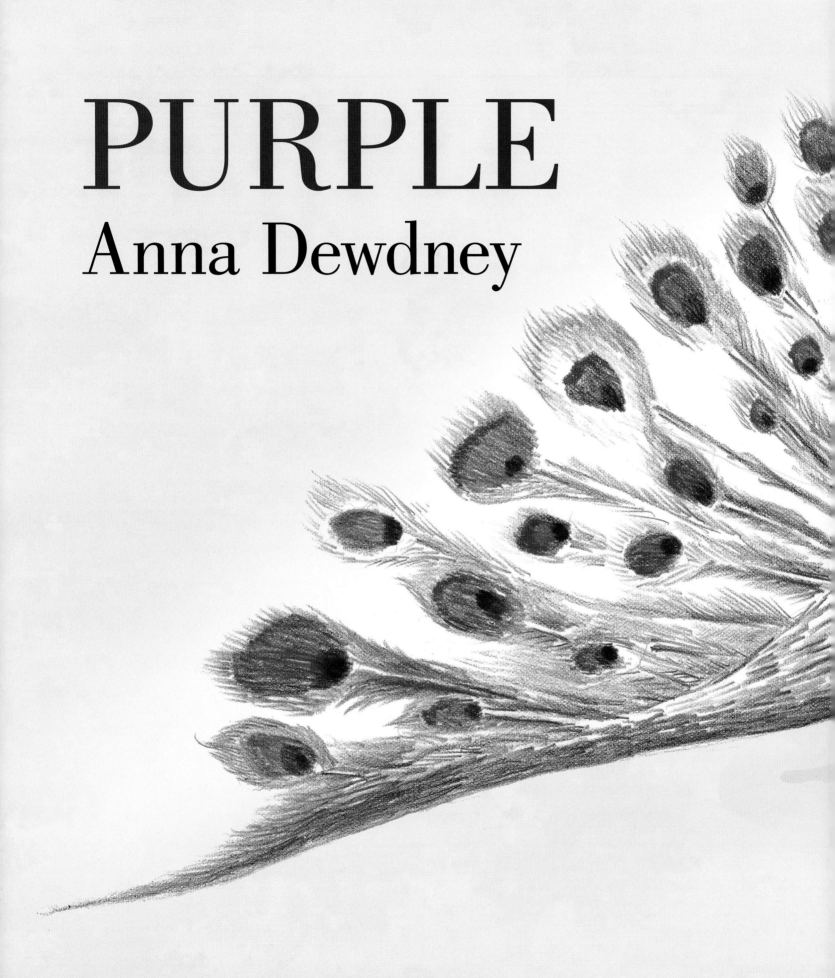

When I was a little girl, my favorite outfit was my purple polyester pantsuit, and I wanted purple peacocks in the front yard. When I grew up, I got them.

GRAY

RAFAEL LÓPEZ

The color I choose will surprise you because it dares to be different. No matter what others may say, artists know that gray is magic. It gets along with all the other colors and knows how to make them sparkle. Gray is smart and UNIQUE!

Like the clever octopus, my good friend gray knows how to change colors to communicate. It comes in many different shades—from warm to really cool! In some parts of the world, this flexible color even changes its spelling to *grey*.

When things get noisy and mixed up, gray is like a calm, deep breath.

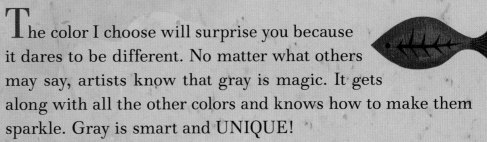

WHITE

Lauren Castillo

I love the way snow magically paints the world white.

GREEN

Philip C. Stead

A green frog is green
and sometimes socks are green—
just like yarn.
An alligator is green
unless it hides underwater
and then it's
two   white   eyes.
Green grass is green
and apples can be green.
A tree is green
except when it's yellow
red
or nothing at all.
You know what?
A green elephant is green
when it wants to be
and that's why today
my favorite color
is green.

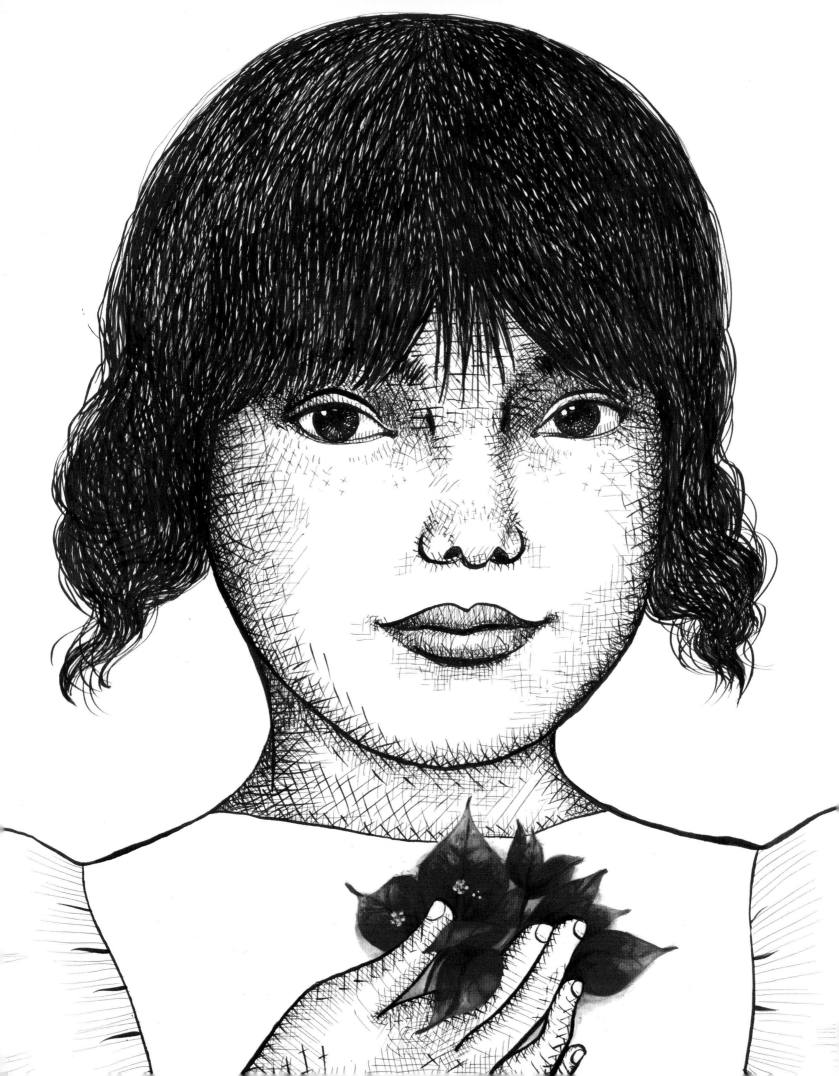

Mexican Pink
Yuyi Morales

Fiery, intense, and alive is
Mexican Pink, the color
of bougainvillea flowers I
used to cut on my way
to visit my grandmother
when I was a child.

MAINE MORNING GRAY

Melissa Sweet

<u>Haiku for Gray</u>

Foggy morning gray
makes other colors glimmer.
Even the gull's beak.

- - -   fog gray

——   silver gray

——   grey gray

- - -   charcoal gray

⊢   seagull gray

➞   granite gray

- -   pencil gray

—   spruce gray

- - -   anchor gray

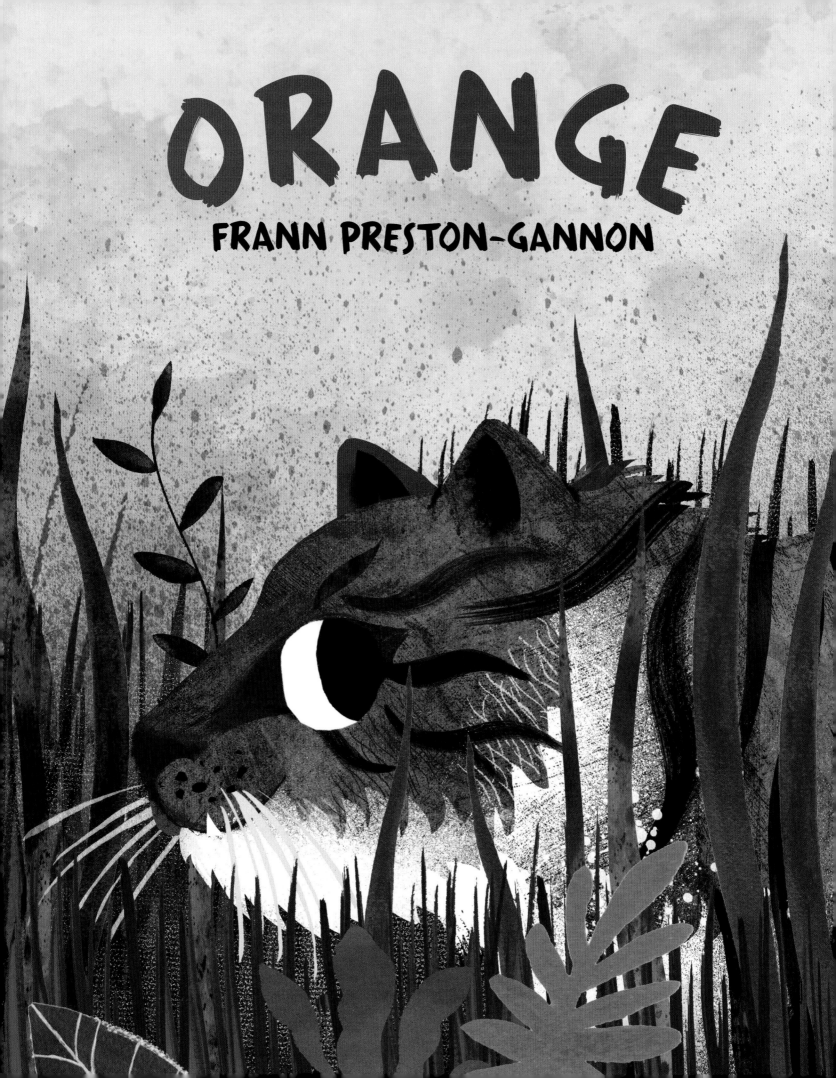

I love **flaming orange**. It is the color of the tiger burning bright as it creeps through the grasses of the jungle.

BLACK

Jill McElmurry

Sometimes I imagine a place called the Black Garden. It's my own private garden, lush with trees and flowers that are dark and velvety. It's quiet and cool, even on hot days. It's wild and mysterious but feels safe. The Black Garden is where I go to get lost in my thoughts, dance around, have a good cry, sing a song, paint a picture, or maybe eat a slice of dark chocolate cake. The Black Garden is unpredictable. The Black Garden is the garden of me.

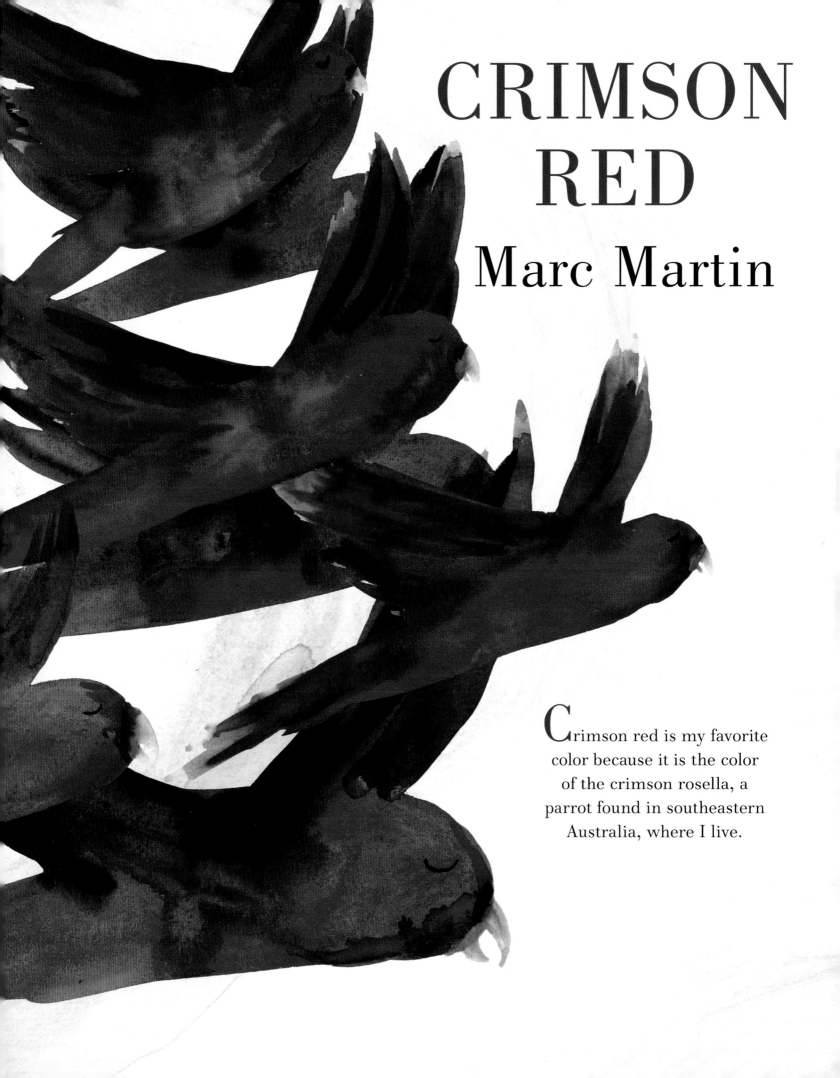

CRIMSON RED

Marc Martin

Crimson red is my favorite color because it is the color of the crimson rosella, a parrot found in southeastern Australia, where I live.

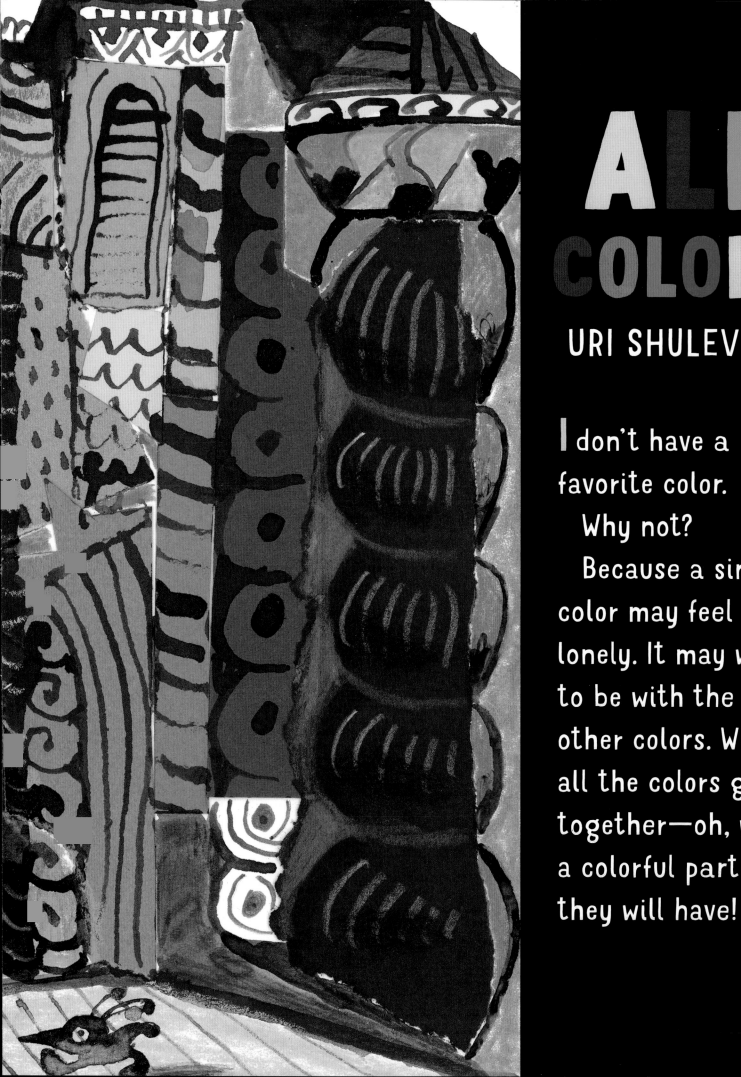

ALL
COLORS

URI SHULEVITZ

I don't have a
favorite color.
Why not?
Because a single
color may feel
lonely. It may want
to be with the
other colors. When
all the colors get
together—oh, what
a colorful party
they will have!

Eric Carle is the author and illustrator of more than seventy books, including *The Very Hungry Caterpillar* and *Brown Bear, Brown Bear, What Do You See?* written by Bill Martin Jr. Eric was born in the United States but spent his early years in Stuttgart, Germany, where he studied art and design at the Academy of Applied Art. [eric-carle.com]

Bryan Collier grew up in Pocomoke City, Maryland. His first book, *Uptown*, won the Coretta Scott King Award for illustration and the Ezra Jack Keats New Illustrator Award. He has since received many other awards and honors, including five Coretta Scott King Awards and three Caldecott Honors. [bryancollier.com]

Mike Curato is the author and illustrator of the Little Elliot series and has illustrated a number of other books for children, including *Worm Loves Worm* by J. J. Austrian and *All the Way to Havana* by Margarita Engle. You can find him on any given day walking around, eating a cupcake (or thinking about it). [mikecurato.com]

William Low is an educator, lecturer, author, and illustrator. He likes to paint, spend time with his family, and, when things are quiet, run around his old house looking for things to fix. He has illustrated numerous adult and children's books, including those by John Steinbeck, Ernest Hemingway, and Maeve Binchy; his illustrations also appear in Bill O'Reilly's *The Last Days of Jesus*. He has authored and illustrated several picture books for Henry Holt, including *Chinatown*, *Old Penn Station*, *Machines Go to Work in the City*, and *Daytime Nighttime*. [williamlow.com]

Etienne Delessert is a Swiss-American artist and author; his picture books have earned numerous honors, among them two Graphic Prizes from the Bologna Children's Book Fair. He was twice nominated for the Hans Christian Andersen Award and had retrospectives of his work at the Louvre and at the Library of Congress in Washington, D.C. Among his many children's book credits are *Stories 1, 2, 3, 4* by Eugène Ionesco; *I Hate to Read!* by Rita Marshall; *Ashes Ashes*; *Night Circus*; and *Fuzzy, Furry Hat*. [etiennedelessert.com]

Anna Dewdney (1965–2016) was the bestselling author and illustrator of more than fifteen award-winning children's books, most notably the Llama Llama series. Her stories have been adapted into several theater productions and translated into more than ten foreign languages. Anna grew up outside New York City and lived in Vermont, where she enjoyed running, gardening, and spending time with her two daughters and several dogs. Anna was a strong advocate and spokesperson for literacy. She believed in the power of sharing stories and reading together. Anna said it best herself in an essay for *The Wall Street Journal*: "When we open a book, and share our voice and imagination with a child, that child learns to see the world through someone else's eyes." [llamallamabook.com]

The work of **Rafael López** is a fusion of strong graphic style and magical symbolism. Growing up in Mexico City, he was immersed in rich cultural heritage and colorful surroundings. He is the recipient of two Pura Belpré Medals for illustration, for *Drum Dream Girl* by Margarita Engle and *Book Fiesta!* by Pat Mora. He has received three additional Pura Belpré Honors and two Américas Awards for illustration. In 2012 he was selected by the Library of Congress to create artwork for the National Book Festival in Washington, D.C. [rafaellopez-books.com]

Lauren Castillo studied illustration at the Maryland Institute College of Art and received her MFA from the School of Visual Arts in New York City. She has written and illustrated numerous books for children, including *Twenty Yawns* by Jane Smiley, *Yard Sale* by Eve Bunting, *The Reader* by Amy Hest, and *Happy Like Soccer* by Maribeth Boelts. One of her most recent books, *Nana in the City*, was awarded a 2015 Caldecott Honor. She currently draws and dreams in Harrisburg, Pennsylvania. [laurencastillo.com]

Philip C. Stead is the author of the 2011 Caldecott Medal winner, *A Sick Day for Amos McGee*, as well as *Bear Has a Story to Tell*, an E. B. White Honor book. Books that he has written and illustrated include *Creamed Tuna Fish & Peas on Toast*; *Jonathan and the Big Blue Boat*; *A Home for Bird*; *Hello, My Name Is Ruby*; and *Sebastian and the Balloon*. Philip lives with his wife, illustrator Erin E. Stead, in Northern Michigan. [philipstead.com]

Yuyi Morales is an author, artist, and puppet maker and was the host of her own Spanish-language radio program for children. She has won numerous awards, including the Jane Addams Award, five Pura Belpré Medals, and three Pura Belpré Honors. Long a resident of the Bay Area, she now resides in Veracruz, Mexico, where she was born. [yuyimorales.com]

Melissa Sweet is the author of many award–winning children's books. She wrote and illustrated *Some Writer! The Story of E. B. White* and illustrated two Caldecott Honor books: *A River of Words: The Story of William Carlos Williams* and *The Right Word: Roget and His Thesaurus*, both by Jen Bryant. She lives on the coast of Maine and looks forward to foggy mornings. [melissasweet.net]

Frann Preston-Gannon is a London-based illustrator and author of books for children. In 2011 she was awarded the Sendak Fellowship, which allowed her to spend a month living and working with the great master of illustration Maurice Sendak at his home in Connecticut. Since then, her books have been published around the world and have received numerous awards. Her latest titles include *Dave's Cave*, *Because of an Acorn*, and *My World*. [frann.co.uk]

Jill McElmurry was born in Los Angeles to a family of artists and musicians. Before fulfilling her lifelong dream of creating picture books, Jill illustrated magazines, book covers, posters, and design projects in the United States and Germany; she's had several pieces shown at the Society of Illustrators. When she's not working on books, she's painting the New Mexico landscape or enjoying herself with her partner, Eric, and their dog, Harry, in beautiful Taos, New Mexico. [jillmcelmurry.com]

Marc Martin is an artist, illustrator, and picture-book maker based in Melbourne, Australia. He is the author and illustrator of numerous picture books, including *A Forest*, *The Curious Explorer's Illustrated Guide to Exotic Animals A to Z*, *Max*, *A River*, and *LOTS*. Marc's work is a world of dense color, rich textures, and the odd scribble. He draws inspiration from his surroundings, nature, and the city he lives in. [marcmartin.com]

Uri Shulevitz, a Caldecott Medal–winning illustrator and author, was born in Warsaw, Poland. He began drawing at the age of three and, unlike many children, never stopped. He has earned three Caldecott Honors, for *The Treasure*, *Snow*, and *How I Learned Geography*. His many other books include *One Monday Morning*, *Dawn*, and *So Sleepy Story*. He lives in New York City. [urishulevitz.com]